THINGS TO DO IN AUGUSTA GEORGIA BEFORE YOU DIE

ANBU
TATTOO
ANBU
TATTOO

100 THINGS TO DO IN AUGUSTA GEORGIA BEFORE YOU DIE

TOM MACK

Reedy Press
PO Box 5131
St. Louis, MO 63139, USA
www.reedypress.com

Library of Congress Control Number: 2021935123

ISBN: 9781681063171

Design by Jill Halpin

Author headshot by Michael Budd. All other images by the author.

Printed in the United States of America
21 22 23 24 25   5 4 3 2 1

DEDICATION

This book is dedicated to Michael Budd in celebration of our many happy journeys together.

CONTENTS

Music and Entertainment

Sports and Recreation

Shopping and Fashion

PREFACE

Augusta keeps reinventing itself. Established in 1736 as a British trading post for purchasing commodities from the local Native American population, the town eventually evolved—because of its location on the northernmost point of navigation on the Savannah River—into a market town for agricultural products such as tobacco and cotton. Water power, which was enhanced by the construction of a canal system in 1845, turned Augusta into a leading manufacturing center; its position as a hub for the health sciences and the headquarters of the US Army Signal Corps gave the city a relatively stable economic base.

With the decline of heavy industry and the growth of the suburbs, by the end of the twentieth century many viewed Augusta as a municipality in decline. Only professional golf in the form of the annual Masters Tournament each spring engendered a significant spark of commercial life.

Yet, with a new century and the advent of new technologies, the city may have turned a corner. Cybersecurity is the focus of several new enterprises, and the downtown area is experiencing a revival of sorts with new restaurants and burgeoning nightlife. Augusta's often-hidden charms have been augmented by these fresh developments, and this book focuses on the city's pleasures both steadfast and new.

JAMES R. RANDALL

ACKNOWLEDGMENTS

The writing of this book became an even more enjoyable experience thanks to those fabulous folks who helped me explore all the nooks and crannies of Augusta, making on-site visits to the places outlined herein. First and foremost is Michael Budd, inveterate traveler and life partner. Next are close friends who shared my municipal explorations: Jane Tuten, Cynthia Hazen, Nicholas Stratas, Judi Hammond, James Hammond, Jim Jackson, and Barbara Jackson. Thanks to you all.

FOOD AND DRINK

1

EXPERIENCE THE FOODIE RENAISSANCE ON UPPER BROAD

Foodies have recently discovered the bounty of great places to eat in downtown Augusta, especially on Broad Street between 13th Street and James Brown Boulevard. On most weekend nights, parking is at a premium within close walking distance of these establishments. On local restaurant surveys, Frog Hollow Tavern ranks near the top in the category of fine dining. Open for dinner only, the tavern is noted for its elevated Southern cuisine, artfully presented, and its expansive wine list. Locally and regionally grown ingredients are incorporated into the à la carte entrées and the small plates selections. The environment is upscale, with subdued lighting and discreet service. Frog Hollow is an excellent dining option for a celebratory occasion.

1282 Broad St., 706-364-6906
froghollowtavern.com

TIP

For those in love with Augusta at night, join the crowd on First Friday, a monthly happening when businesses stay open late and the sidewalks are full of happy pedestrians, shoppers, and diners.

2

FEAST ON THE PIG
FAVORED BY A PRESIDENT

Try a taste of the Deep South barbeque that Jimmy Carter served on the White House lawn. Founded by Claude and Adeline Sconyers in 1956, Sconyers Bar-B-Que specializes in pork barbeque cooked in a pit over mesquite coals for twenty-four hours. Patrons can also order beef brisket and tenderloin, chicken, and turkey served with all the fixings in six dining rooms decorated in log cabin style. The traditionally large portions are served by female staff dressed in historic garb. The quality of the food and the attractive setting have made Sconyers a major tourist attraction; the two-story hilltop restaurant is surrounded by carefully landscaped grounds replete with koi ponds. Rated by *People* magazine as one of the ten best barbeque restaurants in the country, Sconyers has carefully maintained its status over time.

2250 Sconyers Way, 706-790-5411
sconyersbar-b-que.com

TIP

Southerners love their pork barbeque, and the Augusta area has many fine establishments serving plenty of grilled meat. An extremely popular newcomer on the barbeque scene is the Southbound Smokehouse, which often features live music.

Augusta
1855 Central Ave., 706-733-5464

North Augusta
1009 Center St., 803-349-9306

southboundsmokehouse.com

3

SAVOR THE CLASSIC DELI EXPERIENCE
AT HILDEBRANDT'S

One of Augusta's oldest businesses, opened by Nicholas Hildebrandt in 1879 as a grocery store with the deli in the back, Hildebrandt's is now run by the fourth generation of the family. True to the motto "Part German, Part South," the business is today devoted almost entirely to food preparation, with a dozen classic sandwiches as its staple menu items. Lu's Choice, for example, is named for current proprietor Luanne Hildebrandt, who was actually born on the second floor of the premises. The sandwich includes turkey, roast beef, ham, hard salami, provolone, and cheddar with mayo and spicy mustard on rye. The emphasis is on the meat and not the bread. Sides vary from day to day, but German potato salad is nearly always available.

226 Sixth St., 706-722-7756
hildebrandtsaugusta.com

TIP

Check out Hildebrandt's assortment of mustards, hot sauces, and honeys for sale. From time to time, patrons can also purchase handcrafted items, such as Christmas ornaments, arranged in old-fashioned display cases on either side of the main dining area. This vintage mercantile establishment has changed its appearance very little over the decades.

4

GO CAJUN AND CREOLE
AT THE FRENCH MARKET GRILLE

If a taste of New Orleans is your objective, the French Market Grille is the perfect destination. The original restaurant in Surrey Center opened in 1983, and it was so popular that a second location in Martinez followed. Traditional Big Easy fare is the name of the game: jambalaya, gumbo, po boys, and crawfish etouffee. Diners' favorites include the chop-shaped crab cake lightly dusted with bread crumbs and the belly-busting peanut butter pie. For those who like their food on the spicier side, there are hot sauces on each table. The ambiance is casual, and the service is friendly.

French Market Grille
425 Highland Ave., 706-737-4865
thefrenchmarketgrille.com

French Market Grille West
360 Furys Ferry Rd., 706-855-5111
frenchmarketwest.com

5

NOSH AND SIP
AT CRAFT AND VINE

Nighttime dining is the name of the game at Craft and Vine, which, as its name implies, specializes in sophisticated alcoholic offerings with some light fare thrown in for good measure. There is an online waiting list for this popular watering hole on Upper Broad, with its long, narrow space configuration, cozy booths on the left and a lengthy bar on the right. It's a perfect upscale date night destination. Menu items change frequently, but you can always count on tasty wood-fired pizzas as well as charcuterie and cheese offerings. The wine selection is large, and the cocktails are inventive.

1204 Broad St., 706-496-8442
craftandvine.com

NIBBLE THE NOBLE WAY

Taking its name from the follower of Georgia founder James Oglethorpe, who laid out the city in 1736, Noble Jones is one of Augusta's newest and most alluring eateries. Customers enter the premises through a courtyard surrounding a bubbling fountain. The capacious dining room features high ceilings; exposed roof beams; brick walls; and a long, curved bar the length of one side of the building. In both setting and menu, owner J. D. Wier has created a dining experience that pays homage to Old Town Augusta. The cuisine matches the decor: casual menu selections imbued with a touch of the unexpected. Customer favorites include smoked fried chicken, Memphis-style spaghetti with pulled pork, hot pepper slaw, and coffee carrots. Whether you order a sandwich, a salad, or a hot entrée, everything is served with an inventive twist.

816 Cotton Ln., 706-305-3344
noblejonesaug.com

"Smoking" is a specialty at Noble Jones. Drinks may come to the table under a bell jar filled with smoke. Try ordering the smoked crab cakes or any dish with one of the restaurant's signature smoked cheeses. The grilled cheese sandwich on buttered French bread, for example, can come with smoked cheddar, Swiss, or blue cheese.

7

SIP AND SURVEY
AT THE CITY'S SIGNATURE DISTILLERY

Opposite the soaring Eighth Street fountain, in a one-story brick building that once stored cotton, is the city's one and only distillery. Named for Augusta's current status, which places the city just behind Atlanta in population, 2nd City Distilling Company is located right next to the Riverwalk. A stop at the tasting room provides a pleasant respite from any outdoor ramble along the Savannah. The interior is surprisingly spacious, with generous seating and an inventive use of barrels for display of the various products that are distilled, bottled, and packaged by hand: bourbon, whiskey, vodka, gin, and rum. The place can be rented for private events. Free tours of the impressive workspace to the side and rear of the building—most last about 20 minutes—can be scheduled in advance.

4 Eighth St., 706-214-2288
secondcitydistilling.com

David Long and Cal Bowie also own Carolina Moon Distillery in Edgefield, South Carolina, the source of a number of popular moonshine variations—some of which, like Rabbit Spit, are also sold at 2nd City. Be sure to stop by!

8

BELLY UP TO THE BAR
AT THE CITY'S BREWERIES

In 2017, Georgia law was amended so breweries and distilleries could begin selling their products for on-site consumption and offering larger quantities for customers to take home. Since then, two major independent breweries have opened in Augusta: River Watch Brewery and Savannah River Brewing Company. They offer different experiences. Situated in a revamped warehouse in the old farmers' market, River Watch Brewery offers primarily outdoor seating. The atmosphere is casual and dog-friendly. Board games and tours are available. Savannah River Brewing Company offers a rotating assortment of hand-crafted beers; but the indoor space (16,000 square feet) is much larger than at River Watch, so the place attracts much bigger crowds. Free tours are conducted by well-informed and enthusiastic guides.

River Watch Brewery
1175 Fourth St., 706-421-7177
riverwatchbrewery.com

Savannah River Brewing Company
813 Fifth St., 706-426-8212
savannahriverbrew.com

TIP

Whether you are an ardent yoga devotee or just a beginner, beer yoga classes are a regular feature on Saturday mornings at the Savannah River Brewing Company. Bring your mat, and they'll supply the beer! One price covers the class and a pint of beer.

9

OBEY YOUR MAMA
AND EAT YOUR VEGETABLES

"Clean Greens in the Dirty South" is the motto of the Southern Salad, which prides itself on serving local, farm-fresh ingredients in commodious bowls. All the lettuce and herbs come from the restaurant's 1,500-square-foot hydroponic greenhouse. Salads are made to order, with each customer choosing the components in four stages. The base can be greens or grains; next comes a choice of nearly 30 toppings of vegetables, legumes, and fruits; the third step involves selecting optional cheeses, proteins, or nuts; finally, the customer picks a dressing. Each salad comes with chips or a jalapeño-cheddar corn muffin. Take-out orders are an option at SoSal, but most customers enjoy dining in this attractive eatery, its bright white walls accented with patches of green AstroTurf.

1008 Broad St., 706-504-4476
thesouthernsalad.com

TIP

The most popular liquid accompaniments are the special smoothies. Try the "creamsicle" blend of coconut yogurt, a whole orange, a banana, and almond milk.

10

FIND WHAT'S LEFT
OF THE FAT MAN

Founded in the 1940s by Horace Usry, the original Fat Man café was for many years part of a year-round "one-of-a-kind" seasonal store that became a local landmark. Fat Man's Forest closed in 2008, but the Usry family moved their restaurant business to the historic Enterprise Mill, where Fat Man's Mill Café offers farm-to-table Southern cuisine in a large, high-ceilinged dining room with exposed brick walls. Southern cuisine and Southern hospitality are the order of the day. The catfish, both fried and blackened, is a particular customer favorite, as is the pot roast. Both table and take-out service are available.

1450 Greene St., 706-733-1740
fatmans.com

TIP

Try the "Real Meal," which includes one meat and a choice of two or three sides. You'll find almost twenty options, including squash casserole, fried pickles, and sweet potato casserole. The sweet corn bread is particularly noteworthy, boasting a texture very similar to cake.

11

SAMPLE ITALIAN CUISINE,
BOTH OLD SCHOOL AND NEW

Augustans have long loved eating Italian. Luigi's, which opened its doors in 1949, was the brainchild of Greek native Nicholas Ballas, whose portrait still hangs at the entrance to the oldest family-owned restaurant in the city. Now managed by the third generation of the Ballas family, the restaurant founded by "Papou Nick" remains a favorite of local residents. The menu features rustic Italian and Greek cuisine served in generous portions; the interior remains unchanged over time, with classic golf mementos on the wall and coin-operated jukeboxes. For a more upscale Italian dining experience, try Ristorante Oliviana in Surrey Center, with its copper ceiling and optional outdoor dining—the craft cocktails are always inventive—and Augustino's in the Marriott on the Riverwalk, with its prime steaks and pasta bar.

Luigi's
590 Broad St., 706-722-4056
luigisinc.com

Oliviana
399 Highland Ave., 706-723-1242
olivianaitaliano.com

Augustino's
2 10th St., 706-823-6521
augustinos.net

12

NEST
AT THE PARTRIDGE INN

From the turn of the twentieth century to World War II, Augusta touted itself as a winter resort, enticing visitors from October to March. The last significant hostelry still extant from that period is the Partridge Inn. What began in the early nineteenth century as a private home opened in 1910 as a hotel, which was extensively renovated in 2014–15 as part of the Curio Collection by Hilton. Famous guests over the years have included music legend Bob Dylan and golfing greats such as Gary Player. Perched on the crest of a hill overlooking the city, the hotel offers great views from its P. I. Bar and Grill, which features indoor and outdoor seating. The decor can best be described as casual elegant, and the cuisine showcases upscale variations on American classics.

2110 Walton Way, 706-737-8888
partridgeinn.com

TIP

Sunday is a special day at the Bar and Grill because of its popular "Best of Augusta" brunch, featuring shrimp and grits and a wide selection of desserts.

13

BUILD THE BEST BURGER

The four-step burger building process at Farmhaus begins with the main ingredient, either a double beef patty composed of a blend of chuck, brisket, and short rib or a double patty of ground turkey, grilled chicken, or Sea Island red peas. Customers then choose from three bun options, seven sauces, and nearly 30 accompaniments, including bacon jam and roasted pork belly. If the build-a-burger choices make you dizzy, there are seven prepared options, including the Haus burger with smoked gouda, grilled onion, and whole-grain mustard. Customers can wash down their burger with fountain drinks or a range of alcoholic options, including boozy shakes. The ambiance is post-industrial, with exposed ductwork overhead and corrugated tin above the bar where orders are taken.

1204 Broad St., 706-496-8771
farmhausburger.com

TIP

This popular burger emporium is also a great place for building your own grilled cheese sandwich. Most of the burger accompaniments can also be ordered with your sandwich, and there are four prepared options, including the Early Bird with smoked gouda, an egg sunny side up, smoked bacon, and Duke's mayo.

14

EXPERIENCE GOOD DEED DINING
AT EDGAR'S

Two Edgar's locations give patrons a chance to dine for a good cause; part of the proceeds go to charity, supporting an outreach program of Goodwill Industries with a focus on the culinary arts. Edgar's Grille has long attracted discriminating diners because of its upscale menu featuring local ingredients and its attractive interior space and courtyard. The new Edgar's Above Broad, an indoor-outdoor eatery on a third-floor rooftop overlooking the heart of the city, promises to be an even more popular gathering place. The two-hundred-seat watering hole is designed to appeal to a younger demographic, with its own bocce ball court, oversized outdoor chess board, and putting green. It's an especially great place for weekend dining before a show at the Miller or the Imperial, both within easy walking distance.

Edgar's Grille
3165 Washington Rd.,
706-854-4700
edgarsgrille.com

Edgar's Above Broad
699 Broad St., Suite 300,
762-320-4320
edgarsabovebroad.com

For fine dining, pick Edgar's Grille. For a more casual indoor-outdoor experience in an urban setting, choose Edgar's Above Broad. Both options help others fulfill their educational goals.

SAVOR MEXICAN CUISINE
WITH A SIDE ORDER OF FUNK

Long a favorite with the younger crowd, Nacho Mama's offers traditional Tex-Mex fare in a downtown space with a decidedly funky flair. Sidewalk dining is an option, but most patrons prefer to eat inside this shotgun-style storefront, whose darkened walls are ablaze with vintage posters and the work of local artists, such as pop musician and painter Billy Sanders ("Billy S"). Orders are taken and delivered at the long left-hand bar; seating is available along the opposite wall or in a large loft space in the back. Specialties include thirteen variations on the classic burrito; in fact, one of the eatery's slogans is "rollin' 'em fat since 1996." Also noteworthy are fourteen different tacos and even more quesadilla options. Dishes featuring the restaurant's signature red chili shrimp are especially popular.

976 Broad St., 706-724-0501
nachomamasaugusta.com

TIP

Try to beat the crowd and claim one of the two tables in what were once display windows on either side of the front entrance. These cozy spaces, on platforms above the main dining area, are excellent spots to see and be seen.

16

SING A HAPPY SONG
AT FINCH AND FIFTH

Noted for its friendly service, Finch and Fifth is an "Americana Bistro" in the upscale Summerville section of Augusta. Established in 2013, the restaurant, located in the second terrace of Surrey Center, prides itself on both its artisanal cheeses and Southern dishes made from local ingredients. The lunch menu boasts at least a half dozen cheese items served a la carte, and all menus—lunch, happy hour, and dinner—feature such traditional Southern fare as boiled peanuts, tomato pies, and Vidalia onion soup. Especially popular are the Southern sliders made of black Angus beef topped with bacon jam and pimento cheese. The atmosphere is casual with both indoor and outdoor seating; the place is especially busy at lunch and at happy hour. Reservations are recommended.

379 Highland Ave., Surrey Center, 706-364-5300
finchandfifth.com

TIP

Second only to the restaurant scene downtown along Broad Street are the dining establishments in Surrey Center. In addition to Finch and Fifth, notable restaurants include Abel Brown Southern Kitchen, Calvert's, Bodega Ultima, and the SolFood Kitchen.

17

JIVE TO JAVA

Coffee roasters and espresso bars have become more than a fad nationwide, and Augusta boasts some of the best. Buona Caffe roasts its coffees on-site and curates espresso drinks with house-made syrups. To accompany the liquid treats, this artisan coffee supplier also serves sandwiches and desserts. Buona Caffe now boasts two locations: one near Augusta University and the other downtown. A downtown fixture since 1999, Metro Coffeehouse and Pub offers hand-crafted espressos and blends by day and alcoholic beverages by night. So popular was its Aiken location that the New Moon Café opened another, equally appealing destination in downtown Augusta. House-made coffees and pastries are served in a bohemian atmosphere featuring displays of local art.

Buona Caffe
1858 Central Ave., 706-869-4074
1 11th St., 706-432-9136
buonacaffe.com

Metro Coffeehouse and Pub
1054 Broad St., 706-722-6468

New Moon Café
936 Broad St., 706-823-2008
newmoondowntown.com

18

"GO-GO"
TO WHISKEY BAR KITCHEN

Two hundred whiskeys from seven whiskey regions around the world are the inspiration for this watering hole founded by brothers Kenny and Bobby Morrison. The indoor dining space is long, dark, and narrow, with a bar on the left and tables and booths on the right against an exposed brick wall; outside on the street are picnic tables under a capacious overhang punctuated with ceiling fans. The food menu features an unusual combination of Japanese-inspired entrées and small plates, as well as American comfort food, including a dozen craft burgers. The eatery is particularly popular at lunch. Reservations are not accepted, but you can ascertain the wait time by accessing the website.

1048 Broad St., 706-814-6159
whiskeybarkitchen.com

TIP

Vegetarians will find a wide variety of menu items from which to choose, including the highly popular seaweed salad and the garlic butter/whiskey edamame. In addition, the beef in all the burgers can be substituted with veggie patties.

19

WATCH DAY TURN TO NIGHT
AT SOLÉ AUGUSTA

Fast becoming one of the most popular downtown eateries, Solé offers a festive dining experience that bridges the daylight and nighttime hours. Indoor dining is available in two large interior spaces, but the outdoors come alive at night when a two-story patio takes center stage. Large tables with central firepits offer a unique dinner setting after dark; on weekends, the upper patio is active from 10 p.m. until 2 in the morning with craft libations and live music. Small plates are the order of the day, with house-ground burgers a customer favorite as well as a wide variety of sushi. There is also a kids' menu; in fact, at dinnertime, whole families, young and old, can be seen at the restaurant. "Late night," however, the place is taken over by discriminating young adults.

1033 Broad St., 706-432-9898
soleaugusta.com

20

RELISH THE HOSPITALITY
AT PINEAPPLE INK TAVERN

One of Augusta's newest eateries, Pineapple Ink Tavern takes its cue from the two parts of its unusual name. The pineapple has long symbolized a friendly reception, and the ink refers to the copious wall paintings, most by local tattoo artists, to be found there. The darkened interior is welcoming, with both table and booth options; sidewalk dining is also available. Good service is the hallmark of Pineapple Ink, and so is the innovative seasonal cuisine. Autumn fare features, for example, the Sleepy Hollow with spiced roasted pumpkin, dried red fruit marmalade, and taleggio on black Russian rye; winter ushers in a tasty roasted tomato soup. Sammies, mac bowls, and salads are always on the menu.

1002 Broad St., 706-842-4401
pineappleinktavern.com

21

INDULGE IN THE PLEASURES OF SOUTHERN PIZZA AT THE PIZZA JOINT

Is there such a thing as Southern pizza? Perhaps not, although the pie with smoked chicken and white barbeque sauce served at the Pizza Joint comes close. Also on offer are other unusual variations on the traditional pizza pie, all fired in a brick oven, including Sicilian pizza with a fluffy crust and square Detroit-style pizza. An Augusta favorite since 1996, the restaurant does everything from scratch, making its dough and sauces fresh. The Pizza Joint boasts a full bar with nightly specials. The premises serve as an unexpected oasis in the middle of the city's urban core. A grassy pathway between commercial buildings leads to a patio with umbrella-topped tables and then to the no-frills, concrete-floored dining room beyond.

1245 Broad St., 706-774-0037
thepizzajoint.net

MAKE EVERY DAY OKTOBERFEST
AT VILLA EUROPA

Established in 1985–86, Villa Europa is the place to go for German specialties, including schnitzel prepared in a variety of styles: wiener, jager, rahm, and zigeuner. Sauerbraten with dumplings, bratwurst, and beef roulade with spaetzle help round out the menu of traditional German fare. For a tasty appetizer, try the Bavarian fritters made with ground sausage, sauerkraut, and cream cheese covered in bread crumbs, rolled into a ball, and deep fried. All the servings are generous, and the restaurant offers a copious variety of alcoholic beverages. The interior is old school, with dim lighting, plenty of cozy booths, and wall murals, including one of Neuschwanstein, the fantasy castle of Ludwig II of Bavaria. A trellised deck provides an attractive outdoor dining option.

3044 Deans Bridge Rd., 706-798-6211
villaeuropa.com

TIP

Try Oktoberfest at Villa Europa with live music, boots of beer, and the notorious chicken dance!

23

EXPLORE UPSTAIRS AND DOWN

AT THE CROWNE PLAZA

The newest luxury hotel in the Augusta area, the Crowne Plaza, offers two dining options. Salt + Marrow Kitchen on the first floor serves elevated Southern cuisine in a sophisticated setting featuring black and taupe walls and subdued lighting. Breakfast and lunch are available in the parlor bar, and dinner is served in the adjacent dining room. Among the most popular items are sweet potato bisque, Carolina rice risotto, and local wild-caught shrimp with grits. Jackson's Bluff, the hotel's rooftop bar, offers snacks and a pleasing assortment of alcoholic beverages along with panoramic views of the Augusta skyline and the Hammond's Ferry neighborhood of North Augusta. The bar's name pays tribute to an imaginary promontory from which James U. Jackson, founder of the North Augusta Land Company, might have inspected his brainchild in 1890.

The Crowne Plaza
1060 Center St., North Augusta, 803-349-8400
Salt + Marrow Kitchen
803-349-8401
crownenorthaugusta.com

24

FIND AN ALTERNATIVE TO HOME COOKING
AT WIFESAVER

Though its presence on the local scene has diminished over the years, WifeSaver is still an Augusta area favorite for Southern fried chicken. The company's sexist moniker has failed to change with our evolving notions regarding gender roles—the Cunningham family started the restaurant in 1965—and there is nothing new about the recipes, which have stood the test of time better than the restaurant's name. Other items that remain menu staples include Southern fried steak and fried okra. The first restaurant on Milledgeville Road is long gone, but there are still three locations in Augusta and one each in North Augusta and Grovetown. The sites vary considerably in ambience, and there is also some variance in menu items. The most updated venue is the Furys Ferry Road location.

wifesaverrestaurants.com

25

ENJOY FARM-TO-TABLE DINING
AT MANUEL'S BREAD CAFÉ

A classic farm-to-table restaurant, Manuel's is the inspiration of Manuel Verney-Carron, who assumed responsibility for the sustainable community vegetable garden at Hammond's Ferry, a charming mixed-use neighborhood on the North Augusta side of the Savannah. That French-inspired garden, christened Blue Clay Farm, features flowers, herbs, and vegetables from which the café gathers its supply of table greens each day. Serving lunch and dinner, the café offers both indoor and outdoor dining, the latter on the sidewalk of this corner restaurant in the heart of Hammond's Ferry. Specialties include salmon cake with roasted aioli dressing and Manuel's "famous fries," dipped in a poutine gravy.

505 Railroad Ave., North Augusta, 803-380-1323
manuelsbreadcafe.com

Space is at a premium in the L-shaped dining area inside Manuel's; a welcome alternative is sidewalk dining under a projecting roof with ceiling fans. On sunny days, the restaurant makes use of colorful table umbrellas and waterproof tarpaulins stretched like canvas sails to shield diners from the sun.

MILLER
TOGETHER
WE ARE Music
TOGETHER
WE ARE Music
MILLER

MUSIC
AND ENTERTAINMENT

"GET ON DOWN"
WITH THE GODFATHER OF SOUL

Although James Brown was born in South Carolina, most fans of the "hardest-working man in show business" associate him with the city where he was raised and where he subsequently ran most of his business enterprises. The James Brown Family Historical Tour, run by the James Brown Family Foundation, takes patrons to places in the city that played a large part in the performer's legendary career. The tour includes admission to the Augusta Museum of History, whose Brown exhibit is covered elsewhere. A major selfie site is the statue that Brown himself had a hand in designing shortly before his death in 2006. Located on Broad Street between Eighth Street and James Brown Boulevard, the nearly life-size statue depicts the famous entertainer holding a microphone stand in both hands.

Tour: 560 Reynolds St., 803-640-2090
jbtour.jamesbrownfamilyfdn.org

TIP

Get up close to the sculptural image that captures the entertainer basking in applause. Brown himself requested that the statue not be placed on a plinth; he wanted it to be at street level to encourage fan interaction.

EXPERIENCE SOUTHERN SOUL
AT THE IMPERIAL

A couple of years after a fire destroyed twenty-five blocks in the downtown area, the Imperial Theatre, originally named the Wells, opened on Broad Street. In the years following its 1918 debut, the eight-hundred-seat theater featured vaudeville performances and the projection of what were then called photoplays. Undergoing gradual restoration, the Imperial remains open for business. A highlight of the concert season is the Southern Soul series, sponsored by the Morris Museum of Art since 2003 as part of its mission to showcase all aspects of the Southern cultural experience, not just fine art but music too. Noteworthy jazz, bluegrass, country, and gospel performers are regularly showcased on the Imperial stage.

749 Broad St., 706-722-8341
imperialtheatre.com

TIP

Schedule a backstage tour of the theater that James Brown frequently used as a tryout space for his many worldwide tours.

ROCK YOUR WORLD
AT THE MILLER

Founded in 1940 by Frank Miller as a venue for vaudeville shows and motion picture projection, the Miller Theater reopened in 2018 as a fully restored Art Deco/Art Moderne performing arts center boasting more than 1,200 seats. The lobby features Italian marble terrazzo flooring and black walnut trim; the stage is framed by iconic hand-painted panels celebrating wine and women and implying the accompaniment of song. Stars who have appeared on stage at the Miller include Montgomery Clift, Tallulah Bankhead, and the legendary acting duo of Alfred Lunt and Lynn Fontanne. The film *The Three Faces of Eve* had its premiere at the Miller. The performance schedule alternates concerts by the Augusta Symphony Orchestra, for whom the theater is its principal venue, with shows from major figures in the worlds of rock and roll, folk, and jazz.

708 Broad St., 706-842-4080
millertheateraugusta.com

29

PONDER THE WONDERS OF WESTOBOU

Even before the Savannah Indians were resident in the river valley that now bears their name, the warlike Westos confronted the first European traders who ventured into this part of the country. That original Native American population inspired the name of the multi-arts festival held each year in Augusta. Conceived in 2005 as a five-day showcase of music, dance, film, visual arts, and spoken word, the Westobou Festival adopted the original name of the great river—"the river of the Westos"—to epitomize the flow of artistic creativity across genres. With a central mission focused on diversity and creative exchange, the festival takes place throughout the city in venues large and small, traditional and experimental. The year-round gallery on Broad Street inspired by the festival is covered elsewhere.

1129 Broad St., 706-755-2878
westouboufestival.com

ENJOY ONE MAN'S LEGACY IN CLASSICAL MUSIC

Augusta is the joyful beneficiary of two longstanding classical music organizations founded by one man, the late Harry Jacobs. He established the Augusta Symphony Orchestra in 1954 and the Harry Jacobs Chamber Music Society in 1990. Founding chair of the music department at Augusta University, Jacobs was a major figure in the musical life of the city, as was his wife, Vola, a talented pianist and keyboard instructor. Their devotion to music has had lasting consequences. Each year at the Maxwell Performing Arts Theatre at Augusta University, the Harry Jacobs Chamber Music Society offers five concerts by small instrumental ensembles with world-class reputations. Season subscriptions are available, as are tickets for individual performances.

2500 Walton Way, 706-731-7971
augusta.edu/harryjacobs

31

ENJOY TOWN AND GOWN ENTERTAINMENT

AT THE MAXWELL PERFORMING ARTS THEATRE

Although dramatic productions and musical performances featuring Augusta University students take center stage at the Maxwell Performing Arts Theatre, this 740-seat venue has since 1968 brought to the city artists from across the nation and around the world. Touring companies, ensembles, and individual artists are periodically showcased thanks to the five-event Lyceum Series and the Jacobs Chamber Music Series. The semicircular seating configuration, which surrounds the thrust stage, helps make every seat a good seat. Series subscriptions are available, as well as individual tickets for most performances.

2500 Walton Way, 706-667-4100
augusta.edu/maxwelltheatre

TIPS

Sign up for the digital newsletter *Jagwire Events Weekly* to get the latest news on upcoming events at the Maxwell.

Check out the bronze sculpture in front of the theater. The work of Kathleen Girdler, *Cultural Triad* is composed of three abstract figures representing art, drama, and music.

EXPERIENCE THE FULL ORCHESTRAL SOUND

OF THE AUGUSTA SYMPHONY

One of the oldest cultural organizations in the city, the Augusta Symphony Orchestra has been a regional musical mainstay for nearly seventy years. Now under the baton of Dirk Meyer, its fourth musical director, the orchestra provides concerts at three area venues. Classical and pops concerts are performed at the restored Miller Theater on Broad Street, chamber concerts at the Knox Music Institute in a former department store next door to the Miller, and family concerts at the Hardin Auditorium in Evans. Whatever the venue or configuration, audiences are sure to enjoy one of the country's best regional orchestras.

1301 Greene St., 706-842-4080
augustasymphony.com

DISCOVER ROOTS MUSIC
AT THE BLIND WILLIE MCTELL MUSIC FESTIVAL

As a singer and guitarist, Georgia native Blind Willie McTell (1898–1959) was a twentieth-century pioneer in ragtime and blues music. A street performer in Augusta and Atlanta, McTell made some early recordings but did not live long enough to enjoy the major commercial interest in roots music by the end of the last century. However, he did influence the work of others, including Bob Dylan and the Allman Brothers Band. "Statesboro Blues" and "Broke Down Engine Blues" are perhaps his most popular compositions. Each spring for nearly thirty years, the City of Thomson, just thirty miles west of Augusta, has celebrated McTell's legacy with a family-friendly outdoor festival, which runs from noon to nightfall.

1021 Stagecoach Rd., Thomson, 706-597-1000
blindwillie.com

"GET YOUR GROOVE ON"
AT LIVE MUSIC VENUES AROUND TOWN

Nightclubs in any urban area seem to come and go, their popularity waxing and waning. Such is true of Augusta, which boasts a rotating assortment of after-hours establishments where you can snack, sip, and listen to live entertainment. One downtown nightspot, however, has sustained its boast of "keeping Broad Street funky since 1995." The Soul Bar offers perhaps the most nights of live entertainment downtown, as well as themed nights devoted to the legacy of James Brown. A popular newcomer on the scene is the Loft, a storefront space with a large stage and dance floor; there is karaoke on weeknights and live acts on the weekend. Other top contenders in this category, Edgar's Above Broad and Solé Augusta, are described in the dining section of this book.

Soul Bar: 984 Broad St., 706-724-8880
soulbar.com

Loft: 927 Broad St., 706-828-6600
facebook.com/loftaugusta

ENJOY A DATE NIGHT
AT THE LADY A PAVILION

Dave Haywood and Charles Kelley, two-thirds of the country music group Lady Antebellum, grew up in Evans, just ten miles northwest of Augusta; they graduated from Lakeside High School, class of 2000. Although they eventually moved to Nashville, both were honored by their hometown in 2011 with the naming of an entertainment pavilion in Evans Towne Center Park. After the group changed the word "Antebellum" to the letter "A" in 2020 to disassociate their name from a particular period of Southern history, Evans government officials followed the lead of Lady A in renaming the venue. Public performances continue to attract large audiences to this open-air facility that features a large stage topped with a fan-shaped roof that thrusts forward toward the grass-covered audience space.

7016 Evans Towne Center Blvd., Evans, 706-650-5005

TIP

Try out the other amenities of Evans Towne Center Park. The recreation area features a large playground for children, a walking path, a dog park, and playing fields for Frisbee and football.

36

RUB SHOULDERS WITH BIG STARS

AT THE AUGUSTA ENTERTAINMENT COMPLEX

The Augusta Entertainment Complex includes two significant venues, the 8,000-seat James Brown Arena and the 2,800-seat William B. Bell Auditorium. Collectively the complex boasts the biggest ticket sales in Georgia outside of the Atlanta metropolitan area. Big stars who have played Augusta include Bon Jovi, Diana Ross, Van Halen, KISS, and the Beach Boys. The complex is also home to the annual Augusta Blues Festival and the Broadway in Augusta series. In recent surveys, patrons particularly praise the acoustics at the Bell Auditorium. Parking is available in lots on Seventh and Eighth streets; fees are cash only.

James Brown Arena
601 Seventh St.

Bell Auditorium
712 Telfair St.

706-722-3521
augustaentertainmentcomplex.com

Sign up for the Augusta Entertainment Complex Fan Club to receive information on upcoming shows, as well as exclusive presales and discounts. Even more perks are available by joining the exclusive Windsor Club.

37

FIND YOUR ART IN THE HEART

Managed each year by the Greater Augusta Arts Council, Arts in the Heart of Augusta festival is the biggest public arts event in the city. Spanning four blocks on Broad Street and the Augusta Common, this 2.5-day event each fall comes in three parts: a fine arts and craft market featuring painting, photography, jewelry, textiles, stained glass, woodwork, and ceramics; a global village of food vendors, representing approximately twenty different cultures; and five stages offering performances of music, dance, and the spoken word. On offer are plenty of activities for children, including face painting, various craft projects, and a special scavenger hunt. Scores of street performers, most in costume, are also happy to interact with younger folk.

706-826-4702
artsintheheart.com

TIP

Subscribe to the digital newsletter of the Greater Augusta Arts Council for festival updates.

38

MARCH, DANCE, AND HAVE A GOOD TIME
AT AUGUSTA PRIDE

Celebrate diversity at Augusta Pride. Founded more than ten years ago to promote acceptance of and continuing support for the city's LGBTQ community, this annual event is customarily scheduled for the last weekend in June, the anniversary of the beginning of the modern gay civil rights movement marked by the Stonewall Riots in New York City in 1969. The main events include a parade and giant outdoor party. The parade route encompasses three blocks of Broad Street, concluding at the Augusta Common, the setting for the large block party featuring live entertainment and a host of vendors. Augusta Pride offers a lot of fun for people of all sexual identities.

762-233-5313
prideaugusta.org

39

FOLLOW IN THE FOOTSTEPS OF AN EIGHTEENTH-CENTURY NATURALIST

In his treks through the American Southeast in the 1770s in search of unidentified flora and fauna, naturalist William Bartram spent one unforgettable night sleeping in the upper branches of a tree while hungry gators prowled below. Anyone wishing to follow in Bartram's footsteps today need not worry about such hazardous sleeping accommodations. In fact, most of the seventy-five-mile route mapped out for today's tourists can be navigated by car. Several areas can, however, still be experienced on foot. Nearly nine miles of trail can be found along the Georgia shore of Clarks Hill Lake. Augusta, which Bartram predicted would become the "metropolis of Georgia," commemorates the visit of the man the Cherokee called "the flower hunter" with a marker on the Riverwalk and an exhibit at the Augusta Museum of History.

40

EXPERIENCE THE CSRA'S NEWEST INDOOR PERFORMING ARTS CENTER

With a cost of $35 million, the Columbia County Performing Arts Center opened its doors in 2021. The newest such complex in the Central Savannah River Area, the center on the plaza at Evans Towne Center contains a 2,000-seat auditorium, a space for a museum dedicated to local history, and a multipurpose room for private events. The center has been labeled a "five-truck venue" because its loading docks can accommodate up to five tractor trailers full of the stage sets, props, and other items that touring companies need to put on large-scale performances.

Proponents of the center hope it will serve as a magnet for Broadway touring companies and other top-notch acts, such as those featured at the Peace Center in Greenville, South Carolina.

1000 Market St., Evans, 706-447-6767
thecenterofcc.com

SPORTS AND RECREATION

BUZZ LIKE A GREENJACKET

What do you get when you cross a common predatory wasp with the member jacket at the Augusta National Golf Club? You get the logo of Augusta's minor league baseball team, the GreenJackets, which recently found a new home across the river in South Carolina. The class A affiliate of the Atlanta Braves plays in a nearly 5,000-seat stadium that opened in 2018 in North Augusta. SRP Park features a 360-degree concourse, including a kids' zone and a broad terrace overlooking the Savannah River. Concessions are available from several restaurants and food stores in the stadium itself; patrons can dine in at the Southbound Smokehouse, rated one of the area's best barbeque restaurants, or have fare delivered to their seat or hospitality suite.

187 Railroad Ave., North Augusta, 706-736-7889
milb.com/augusta

TIP

For group outings, the park offers three sizes of private, climate-controlled spaces, ranging from 300 to 4,000 square feet. Guests can enjoy the game inside the well-appointed lounges or outside on the adjoining terraces.

TAKE A CLASS
AT THE GERTRUDE HERBERT

Established in 1937 as the home of the Augusta Arts Club, the non-profit Gertrude Herbert Institute of Art was named after the deceased daughter of the club's greatest benefactor. The Institute offers a host of studio classes for children, teens, and adults in a wide variety of media. The classroom work of local instructors is often augmented by special lectures by visiting artists. Students and casual visitors alike can enjoy the regularly scheduled juried exhibitions on the first and second floors.

506 Telfair St., 706-722-5495
ghia.org

TIP

Don't miss the opportunity to explore the mansion itself, built in 1818 by US Senator Nicholas Ware. Labeled "Ware's Folly" by local citizens for its high cost—its elliptical staircase and elaborate moldings are well worth a gander—the mansion is said to have been the scene of an elaborate ball during an 1825 visit to the city by the Marquis de Lafayette.

43

PLAY A ROUND

COURTESY OF SEVERAL GOLF LEGENDS

If you are not lucky enough to be one of the thousands of visitors who descend on the city each spring brandishing a coveted ticket to the Masters Tournament, there are other, more accessible golfing venues in and around the city that can give you the golf championship experience. Public-access Forest Hills Golf Club, redesigned by Arnold Palmer, was the site of a 1930 tournament win by the legendary Bobby Jones. Two significant private clubs that open their greens during Masters Week are the Palmetto Golf Club in Aiken, designed by Alister MacKenzie, who collaborated with Jones in 1932 on the layout of the Augusta National, and Champions Retreat in Evans, with three courses individually conceived by Jack Nicklaus, Palmer, and Gary Player.

Forest Hills Golf Club
1500 Comfort Rd., 706-733-0001
theforesthillsgolfcourse.com

Palmetto Golf Club
275 Berrie Rd., Aiken, 803-649-2951
palmettogolfclub.net

Champions Retreat
37 Champions Pkwy., Evans, 706-854-6960
championsretreat.net

Reservations are strongly recommended at all three of these courses, especially during Masters Week. For the general public, online applications are required to purchase daily tickets for the Masters Tournament itself; however, only a limited number of purchase applications are accepted each year through a random selection process: Masters.com.

CRUISE THE AUGUSTA CANAL

What role did the town of Lowell, Massachusetts, play in the history of Augusta? Savvy entrepreneurs in Lowell realized that water power could be harnessed to serve heavy industry. In the 1840s, twenty years after the Lowell canal system was constructed, Augusta built its own version. It was widened in the 1870s. Although it no longer generates much hydropower for industry, the canal became a National Heritage Area in 1996 and now serves as a recreational hub for activities on water and land. Visitors can take cruises on the canal in an electric-powered replica of the original, shallow-draft Petersburg boat. The tow path along the canal, level and wide enough for the mules that once propelled canal vehicles, now provides the perfect surface for hiking and biking.

1450 Greene St., Suite 400, 706-823-0440
augustacanal.com

TIP

Plan to enjoy a picnic while navigating the canal. Pack up your own edibles and potables and enjoy one of the packaged tours beginning at the interpretive center in the old Enterprise Mill: the hour-long history and nature tour or the Civil War tour. Weekend music cruises with live entertainment can also be booked, but these ninety-minute floating concerts are so popular that early reservations are suggested.

45

TAKE A GUIDED TOUR
THROUGH LOCAL HISTORY

Because of its essential identity as a commercial and industrial center, Augusta never shared in the glamour of regional municipalities such as Charleston and Savannah. Many of the architectural treasures it did possess were lost, thanks to a belated realization of the benefits of historic preservation. Chartered in 1965, Historic Augusta was founded as a watchdog organization focused on the preservation of the city's "built environment." This nonprofit organization headquartered in the boyhood home of Supreme Court Justice Joseph Lamar offers digital walking tours of Broad, Greene, and Telfair streets. In-person experiences include the annual self-guided Downtown Loft Tour and the equally popular Walk with the Spirits, when guides in period costumes take visitors on a ramble through historic cemeteries.

415 Seventh St., 706-724-0436
historicaugusta.org

46

PARTY AT THE AUGUSTA COMMON

Taking their cue from the sixty acres set aside as common land by town planner Noble Jones in 1736, Augusta's civic leaders decided in 2001 to develop a rectangular greenspace between Broad and Reynolds streets. The new Augusta Common has since served as breathing room in the city's urban core and the setting for a host of community events, including concerts and outdoor festivals. The Broad Street side of the Common features a life-size statue of James Oglethorpe, the founder of Georgia, in civilian attire and as he would have appeared the year the city of Augusta was laid out. The work is by Chicago-based sculptural team Jeffrey Varilla and Anna Koh Varilla.

836 Reynolds St., 706-821-1754
augustaga.gov/1482/augusta-common

SEARCH FOR THE SWAMP THING
AT PHINIZY

Although there have been no verified sightings of the green, humanlike creature showcased in Wes Craven's 1982 horror film, Phinizy Nature Park abounds in wildlife, including alligators and other fauna common to Southern wetlands. The park encompasses 1,100 acres, with fourteen miles of trails. Among the most scenic are the floodplains boardwalk between the parking lot and the visitor center and the equalization pond, which in the fall is nearly smothered in yellow swamp daisies. The park itself is open every day, sunrise to sunset, and free of charge; the visitor center is open only on the weekends. The shop inside the center offers interesting gift items, including pottery and nature prints. Maps can be downloaded from the website or obtained on-site.

1858 Lock and Dam Rd., 706-828-2109
phinizycenter.org

TIP

The park's pleasures vary with the seasons, but it is always wise to wear comfortable shoes and perhaps carry a water bottle and binoculars. Bug spray and sunscreen are advisable during the warmer months.

UNEARTH WHY AUGUSTA HAS BEEN CALLED "THE GARDEN CITY"

In the 1920s, the Chamber of Commerce published a brochure proclaiming Augusta "the Garden City of the South" because it had more "well-planned, carefully planted gardens" than any other locale. The claim was never officially verified, but you can find evidence of Augusta's floral splendor in the heart of the city at the 64-acre Pendleton King Park. Three specialized gardens are particularly noteworthy. In early spring, visitors can ramble down the azalea walk, which ends in the roughly square camellia gardens. The hedge-framed space boasts plants developed at Fruitland Nurseries, the original site of the Augusta National. In late spring, the hydrangea gardens are a must-see because of their complement of seventy varieties. Open seven days a week, dawn to dusk.

1600 Troupe St., 706-564-7462
pendletonkingpark.com

TIP

Children might enjoy a stroll down to the park's retention basin, Lake Elizabeth, where water birds such as the rare Muscovy duck are frequent guests.

49

WITNESS A MAJOR FEAT OF ENVIRONMENTAL SCIENCE
AT BRICK POND PARK

Sometimes saving the environment and having a good time go hand in hand. Designed in the late 1990s to remove pollutants from stormwater runoff on the North Augusta side of the Savannah River, Brick Pond Park is a forty-acre wetland reclaimed from an industrial site devoted largely to brickmaking. Thanks to an artificial waterfall and pumps, the water is now aerated. Special plantings, especially large clusters of fragrant water lilies, have also given the location the look of a traditional Southern wetland. Visitors can hike trails marked by brick-red pebbles, traverse an elevated boardwalk between the two parts of the East Pond, and scan the property from a floating observation deck or fishing platform on the West Pond. A handy trail map is available for download on the website.

88 Georgia Ave.
northaugusta.net

TIP

Picnic tables are located in two scenic spots: near the artificial waterfall on the plant-identification trail and on the causeway between the East and West ponds. You can pack your own picnic or pick up provisions at the Hammond's Ferry Larder. Ample parking can be found in the lot of the North Augusta Municipal Center or in the garage across the street.

50

TAKE A DIP
AT CLARKS HILL LAKE

Located about twenty miles north of Augusta is one of the largest artificial lakes east of the Mississippi. Called Clarks Hill Lake on Georgia maps but designated as Lake Thurmond by the federal government, the 71,000-acre lake was formed by damming the Savannah River in 1951–52. Two state parks on the Georgia side—Elijah Clark and Mistletoe—feature swimming beaches during the summer season. Both parks also offer a host of other amenities, including campsites, picnic shelters, and boat ramps. Lake cruises can be booked on the motor yacht *Seaveyor.* Call 706-614-8402 to book one of the sailing options, such as the highly popular sunset cruise.

Captain & First Mate Services
5577 Marina Pkwy., Appling, 706-614-8402
lakecruisetour.com

TIP

Cast your line! Clarks Hill Lake is touted as one of the best bass fishing areas in the country. Weekend anglers are sure to land "the big one" with a little patience. A Georgia or South Carolina fishing license is required.

RAMBLE
ON THE RIVERWALK

The Riverwalk is a pedestrian zone capitalizing on the city's earthen levee, constructed in 1908 to protect Augusta from river flooding. The brick-paved upper walkway along the top of the old levee runs from Sixth Street to the foot of the 13th Street bridge. About a dozen informational plaques cover topics on both the human and natural history of the area. Highlights of the lower walkway, accessed by cuts in the levee, include the Jessye Norman Amphitheater and the Eighth Street Bulkhead, the site of the popular Saturday market. Both levels afford pedestrians scenic views of the Savannah and the riverfront mansions on the South Carolina side of the river. The Riverwalk also provides an excellent vantage point for major rowing regattas and powerboat races.

TIP

Try out the interactive features on the upper walkway, including the analemmatic sundial cued to Eastern Daylight Time. In this horizontal version, you yourself serve as the gnomon.

52

MIX IT UP
AT THE INTERNATIONAL DISC GOLF COMPLEX

In Appling, Georgia, just twenty-three miles from Augusta, is the international headquarters of the Professional Disc Golf Association, whose grounds feature three demanding courses. The complex has everything you need to get started in the sport: a pro shop and a modern clubhouse where you can watch selections from the association's video archives. There is even a museum! The Headrick Memorial Museum showcases artifacts owned and developed by Ed Headrick, who perfected the design of the Frisbee and earned the title the "Father of Disc Golf." Included is the earliest form of the patented catching device, or "Disc Pole Hole."

3828 Dogwood Ln., Appling, 706-261-6342
pdga.com

TIP

Try other disc golf courses in the Augusta area at Lake Olmstead Park, Pendleton King Park, and Riverview Park.

53

GO BOATING
ON LAKE OLMSTEAD

Formed in the 1870s when Rae's Creek was dammed as part of a larger project to widen the Augusta Canal, the lake has long been a recreational green space in the heart of the urban area. On certain specified days of the week, you can launch either motorized or nonmotorized boats in this eighty-one-acre impoundment. In the past, races were held on its waters. Today flat-bottomed jon boats can most often be seen on the lake, which has a reputation as a good place to catch bass, yellow perch, and crappie.

2205 Broad St.
Kayakaugustacanal.com

TIP

If boating is not your pleasure, tackle either the 3.5-mile walking track covering the rolling terrain around the lake or the disc golf course. Special events also are held periodically in the Julian Smith Casino, named after one of the city's mayors and added to the park in 1936.

54

SIGN UP
FOR A VERY VERA COOKING CAMP

What could be a more classic Augusta experience than an after-hours party during Masters Week? For forty years, local chef Vera Stewart catered such affairs. From that experience has come a host of culinary initiatives, including a television show, blog, and a series of cooking camps. The camps are geared toward children ages six to fourteen. The summer camps involve a generalized introduction to cookery, decorating, and dining etiquette. The fall and spring camps focus mostly on traditional fare associated with specific holidays, such as Halloween, Thanksgiving, and Christmas. In addition to giving the kids hands-on kitchen experience, the staff throws in some life lessons to help ensure each camper's future success.

2708 Wheeler Rd., 706-922-4646
veryvera.com

TIP

Fans of Vera Stewart might want to check out *The Very Vera Cookbook: Recipes from My Table*. Included are directions for making her signature layer cakes, pound cakes, casseroles, soups, and salads.

EXPLORE
HISTORIC SUMMERVILLE

From 1780 to 1912, when it was incorporated into the city of Augusta, Summerville was a separate municipality, known for its splendid private residences. For nearly forty years, the Summerville Neighborhood Association has sponsored a tour of homes, permitting visitors to get a peek inside some of the finest nineteenth- and early-twentieth-century homes in the section of the city popularly known as "The Hill." The tours usually include about eight residences, with friendly guides posted at each location to answer questions and give directions on how to navigate the interior spaces. Photographs are not permitted inside the homes, which offer glimpses of gracious living in what is probably Augusta's most prestigious neighborhood. The area is listed on the National Register of Historic Places.

Summerville Neighborhood Association
P.O. Box 12212, Augusta, GA 30914
summervilleaugusta.com

TIP

Start your tour day at the artisan market, which operates as the tour headquarters and where you can pick up your printed program. Each program contains a handy map and detailed descriptions of the history of each house along with its most distinctive features. Discounted advance tickets can be purchased at specified locations around the city.

56

REACH THE TOP OF YOUR GAME
AT TOPGOLF

New to the Augusta area is an innovative golfing complex called Topgolf. One of fifty such facilities worldwide, Topgolf features high-tech driving ranges. In each of 36 climate-controlled "hitting bays," you can track the flight of your ball digitally on your personal HD screen and play either nine or eighteen virtual holes at such legendary courses as St. Andrews in Scotland and Pebble Beach in Florida. Children might enjoy the nine-hole miniature golf course. Topgolf bills itself as more than just a place to practice your swing. The restaurant, bar, and party patio make it a potential destination for family outings or a full-service location for any golf lover wanting to mark a special occasion with friends.

437 Topgolf Way (just off Riverwatch Parkway), 706-524-0516
topgolf.com/us/augusta

57

VISIT THE TRAINING GROUND OF DOOLITTLE'S RAIDERS

Named for Mayor Raleigh Daniel, who convinced city leaders that Augusta needed an airport, Daniel Field was opened to passenger service in 1931. During World War II, the army took over the property, which was used as a training ground for the pilots in General Jimmy Doolittle's squadron. The short runways mirrored the allotted space on an aircraft carrier. Some of the trainees in Augusta were part of the mission that bombed Tokyo in 1945. Each fall the two-runway field owned by the City of Augusta plays host to the Boshears Skyfest, an air show featuring aerial acrobatics and static displays with special attention to children's entertainment and the potential education of future aviators. Augusta Aviation also provides flight instruction and charter flights. Especially appealing is the thirty-minute sunset flight.

1775 Highland Ave., 706-733-8970
augustaaviation.com

ENJOY A KAYAK TOUR
OF LOCAL WATERWAYS

Based on a student assignment at Augusta University, local resident Cole Watkins established a water-based touring company, Cole Watkins Tours. Specializing in guided tours of the Savannah River and the Augusta Canal, the company offers a variety of waterway experiences, most lasting from two to three hours. Watkins provides the kayak, paddle, and life jacket. Probably the most adventurous tour option features a short hike on Stallings Island, a National Historic Landmark that is accessible only by special permit from the Augusta Archaeological Society. Tour participants get to see a number of shell mounds, inspect prehistoric refuse deposits, and perhaps feed wild donkeys. In addition to conducting tours, Watkins provides kayak rentals.

706-840-0433
colewatkinstours.com

59

PUT THE PEDAL TO THE METAL

AT THE AREA'S PRINCIPAL BIKEWAYS

You don't have to be a champion cyclist to enjoy the Forks Area Trail System (FATS) on the South Carolina side of the Savannah. The system features thirty-four miles of trails and has served as the site of the International Mountain Bicycling Association's World Summit. For a less rigorous challenge, try the paved Greeneway in North Augusta, named after Mayor Thomas W. Greene. This flat, seven-mile circuit encompasses Brick Pond Park and offers glimpses of the Savannah River, the GreenJackets stadium, and other sights in the Hammond's Ferry area. Bicycling is also possible on the eight miles of level towpaths that run along the Augusta Canal on the Georgia side of the river. This trail was once used by draft animals pulling cargo boats upstream from downtown to the locks.

sctrails.net

60

VISIT
A FUNKY LITTLE FLOWER FARM

Celebrated horticulturalist and garden designer Jenks Farmer operates a thriving mail-order business from his home farm in Beech Island, South Carolina, just across the river from Augusta. He and his partner, Tom Hall, specialize in crinum lilies, classic bulb plants in white, pink, rich reds, and stripes. Farmer was the first curator of the Riverbanks Botanical Garden in Columbia and is the former director of the Moore Farms Botanical Garden in Lake City. He is not only a leader in public gardening but also an engaging storyteller. The farm is open to the public on both Mother's Day and Father's Day and for group tours by special arrangement. The house itself dates from the eighteenth century and was later part of the agricultural holdings of nineteenth-century planter and politician James Henry Hammond.

803-386-1866
jenksfarmer.com

TIP

Augustus Jenkins Farmer is the author of two delightful botanical books, *Deep-Rooted Wisdom* and *Funky Little Flower Farm,* as well as an informative digital newsletter. The latter can be accessed through a free subscription, which gets readers on a special mailing list regarding scheduled workshops, lectures, and visiting days.

CULTURE AND HISTORY

61

REVEL IN SOUTHERN ART
AT THE MORRIS

One of only two repositories in the country dedicated to the art of the American South—the other is the Ogden Museum in New Orleans—the Morris Museum of Art is a major attraction on Augusta's Riverwalk. Encompassing two floors in the Augusta Riverfront Center, the museum includes more than ten galleries featuring artworks produced by Southern artists and/or reflecting the culture of the South. In addition to galleries arranged in chronological order from the nineteenth century to the present, there are spaces devoted to specialized subject matter, such as landscape painting. The museum also boasts an attractive gift shop, showcasing catalogs from past exhibitions. Founded by media magnate William Morris III in honor of his parents, the museum opened its doors in 1992. Most special exhibitions are accompanied by informative talks by artists and curators.

1 10th St., 706-724-7501
themorris.org

TIP

Between the first-floor entrance and the auditorium is a 5- by 12-foot photo montage titled *Augusta Allegory* by modern master Robert Rauschenberg. Commissioned by the Morris in 1996, the work incorporates many recognizable downtown buildings and monuments. Visitors will enjoy identifying these local landmarks.

62

DELVE 12,000 YEARS INTO THE PAST
AT THE AUGUSTA MUSEUM OF HISTORY

The Augusta Museum of History provides a shortcut to learning about centuries of life in the Central Savannah River Area. Most of the first floor is taken up with two major exhibit halls. The first is Augusta's Story, which takes visitors from the region's prehistory to the time of the Civil War. Highlights include the reconstruction of a typical village of the Stallings Island Culture and a 56-foot Petersburg boat. The second major space is the Transportation Corridor, dominated by a 1914 steam locomotive pulling a passenger car that can be entered by visitors. Founded in 1937, the museum moved to its current two-story, 10,000-square-foot facility in 1994. The second-floor galleries have received a lot of recent attention, including two small exhibition spaces off the entrance rotunda, both devoted to the local passion for golf.

560 Reynolds St., 706-722-8454
augustamuseum.org

TIP

Don't miss the James Brown exhibit on the second floor, showcasing his bedazzled stage wardrobe and a number of interactive displays, including sound recordings and videos. Even opera lovers will find something of interest: a 2002 film of a duet of Brown's classic "It's a Man's Man's Man's World" with Italian tenor Luciano Pavarotti.

63

EXPERIENCE THE CITY'S MOST SUCCESSFUL REPURPOSED INDUSTRIAL SPACE

A three-story brick textile manufacturing center, Enterprise Mill opened in 1877 and proved a mainstay of the city's industrial vitality for more than a hundred years. Indeed, Augusta was the second largest inland cotton market in the world from the nineteenth century well into the twentieth. With cheaper production costs abroad, however, cotton manufacturing in this country declined. The mill closed in 1983 and remained vacant for more than a decade before local businessman Clayton Boardman purchased the property and converted the mill into a residential complex with office and retail space. Visitors can wander through the Augusta Canal Discovery Center and learn about how the canal solidified the city's role as a major manufacturing center. The shop offers an interesting array of gifts, along with books on Augusta history.

1450 Greene St., 706-774-9220
augustacanal.com

TIPS

As a distinctive souvenir of your visit, pick up a wind chime made from bobbins, the elongated spools used in cotton manufacturing.

The Augusta Canal Discovery Center features interactive exhibits covering the canal's major phases of construction and some of the fine points of its engineering, including peeks at some of the elements that make possible the production of hydroelectric power to this day. Highlights also include a 3D map of the canal and displays that showcase what it was like to work in the mills and live in mill housing.

64

ADMIRE THE WORK
OF A LEADING ABSTRACT SCULPTOR

Driving north on Reynolds, you can't help but spot the gleaming forty-five-foot sculpture that stands as the centerpiece of Springfield Village Park. Dedicated in 2002 as a memorial to one of the earliest African American spiritual communities in the country, *Tower of Aspirations* by Chicago-based sculptor Richard Howard Hunt does indeed embody its title. The stainless-steel construction stretches upward toward the sky like the hopes and prayers of the Baptist congregants who have worshipped just across the street for more than two hundred years. The original church building, constructed in 1801, was rolled on logs from its initial site and donated in the early nineteenth century by the members of what is now St. John United Methodist Church on Greene Street.

1202 Reynolds St.

TIP

Spend some time circumnavigating the 2.5-acre park, with its curvilinear walkways framed by low granite walls. Visitors can stroll around and underneath the principal sculpture, which was joined in 2006 by a second piece by Hunt. Set in the middle of a reflecting pool, this work of welded bronze titled *And They Went Down Both into the Water* is the artist's interpretation of the baptismal encounter between St. Philip and a eunuch. Conveniently placed benches allow for rest and contemplation.

65

EXAMINE MEMORIALS
TO THE COUNTRY'S FOUNDERS

One-tenth the size of the Washington Monument in our nation's capital but of similar obelisk shape, the Signers' Monument on Greene Street marks the final resting place of two of the three Georgia signers of the Declaration of Independence. George Walton and Lyman Hall are entombed beneath the 1848 marble memorial. One of Georgia's two signers of the US Constitution is also buried in downtown Augusta. In anticipation of our country's bicentennial, the remains of William Few were transferred from the abandoned property of the Dutch Reformed Church in Fishkill, New York, to the churchyard of St. Paul's Church on the Riverwalk.

Signers' Monument
500 block of Greene Street

Grave of William Few
St. Paul's Church, 605 Reynolds St.

LEARN MORE ABOUT AUGUSTA'S PRIMARY CONTRIBUTION

TO THE CIVIL WAR

Because of its central location in the Deep South, Augusta lobbied to be the capital of the Confederacy. Although it lost that political campaign, the city was chosen as the site of the largest industrial complex constructed by the South during the war: the Confederate Powder Works. From 1861 to 1865, this manufacturing center, which encompassed twenty-eight structures along the canal, produced 2,750,000 pounds of gunpowder. All that remains today is the 150-foot-tall chimney, which was capped in 1879 as a monumental obelisk; the shaft and castellated base were restored in 2010. The Sibley Mill, constructed in 1882 on the site of the Confederate complex, was built in a neo-Gothic style that mirrors that of the deconstructed powder works.

1717 Goodrich St.

67

RUMINATE OVER AUGUSTA'S MOST SIGNIFICANT MONUMENT

TO THE "LOST CAUSE"

After the capitulation of the Confederacy in 1865, Southerners sought solace in a concept now known as the "Lost Cause." According to this pseudo-historical ideology, the South may have lost the war, but it precipitated the conflict for noble reasons, namely states' rights. Largely ignored was the fact that preservation of the slave economy was the war's principal motivating factor. Thus, in the decades following the Civil War, a number of grand monuments were erected to memorialize the sacrifice of those who had suffered and died. One of the most impressive of these stone memorials is the seventy-six-foot-tall Richmond County Confederate Monument on Broad Street. Four Confederate generals are depicted life-size at the base of the monument. Two are familiar to any history buff: Robert E. Lee and Stonewall Jackson. But the two Georgia-born military leaders are also noteworthy: William H. T. Walker, who is buried on the campus of Augusta University, and Thomas R. R. Cobb, whose home in Athens, Georgia, is now a museum. The enlisted man depicted on top of the monument is Berry Benson, a Confederate sharpshooter who grew up just across the river in North Augusta; he is buried in Sunset Hill Cemetery.

An estimated 10,000 people were in attendance in 1878 when the marble shaft was dedicated.

700 block of Broad Street

68

MARVEL AT THE ONGOING RESTORATION

OF THE HOME OF A FOUNDING FATHER

The object of ongoing restoration by Savannah-based Landmark Preservation LLC is the eighteenth-century residence of George Walton, one of three Georgia signers of the Declaration of Independence. Managed by the Georgia State Society of the Daughters of the American Revolution, Meadow Garden has been open to the public since 1901. But only since 2019 has the house fully revealed its secrets. Today's visitors can now more completely appreciate this unique double domicile. To the left of what was long thought to be the front entrance is the original 1791 residence with its lower roofline; to the right is the larger domestic space constructed after Walton's death in 1804 with its more elevated roofline.

1320 Independence Dr., 706-724-4174
historicmeadowgarden.org

Take the informative tour to witness how the restorers are pulling back the layers of history to reveal a fuller picture of not only one of the oldest house museums in the country but also a building closely associated with one of our country's founders.

EXPERIENCE THE LIFESTYLE

OF AN EIGHTEENTH-CENTURY MERCHANT

In its early days as a river port, Augusta served as a major trading center for two products: cotton and tobacco. In 1794, intent on developing a tobacco brokerage to rival that of Augusta, Ezekiel Harris bought over 300 acres just north of the city where he built a warehouse, constructed a large homestead in 1797 to accommodate not only his family but also planters who arrived with their crops, and established a free ferry on the Savannah to entice business from across the river in his native South Carolina. Touted as one of Georgia's most outstanding eighteenth-century residences, the three-story, wood-frame Ezekiel Harris House is operated today as a museum, offering visitors a chance to experience the lifestyle of a member of the merchant class during the first years of our fledgling republic.

1822 Broad St., 706-722-8454
augustamuseum.org/HarrisHouse

TIP

Purchase your tour tickets at the Augusta Museum of History and save money.

LEARN MORE
ABOUT GEORGIA'S POETIC HERITAGE

In 1913, a monument to four Georgia poets was unveiled on Greene Street. Three have significant Augusta connections. Father Abram Ryan was a priest at St. Patrick's Church and the editor of a Catholic periodical; he was also a celebrated orator whose eloquence is memorialized in Margaret Mitchell's *Gone with the Wind.* James Ryder Randall was editor of the *Augusta Chronicle* and author of Maryland's state song. A splendid statue of Randall also stands in front of Sacred Heart Cultural Center. Paul Hamilton Hayne lived in a modest cottage just outside the city; he was perhaps the South's most important poet and critic during Reconstruction. The most famous of the four, Sidney Lanier, was born and raised in Macon; his most often anthologized composition is "The Marshes of Glynn."

700 block of Greene Street

TIP

A visit to the Four Southern Poets Monument might be paired with a trip to Magnolia Cemetery to see the gravesites of Randall and Hayne.

71

TRACE REMNANTS OF THE OLD ARSENAL

ON THE AUGUSTA UNIVERSITY CAMPUS

In the heart of the Summerville campus of Augusta University are significant remnants of the old Augusta Arsenal, which played a significant part in the military history of our country from 1816 onward. Several structures frame the central quadrangle: the former headquarters building, the former commandant's house, and a guardhouse, which now contains a small museum featuring artifacts that were discovered during campus-based archaeological research. Three Confederate "12-pounder" Napoleon cannons are also displayed on campus. The former commandant's house is now named for author Stephen Vincent Benét, whose father commanded the arsenal from 1911 to 1918. Benét is most famous for "John Brown's Body," an epic poem of the Civil War, which was inspired in part by his residence in Augusta.

2500 Walton Way, 706-737-1632
augusta.edu/admissions/visit.php

TIP

The Summerville campus encompasses two cemeteries, one containing the graves of the soldiers who served at the arsenal and the other containing the graves of members of the Walker family who once owned the summer estate sold to the federal government. The latter section features the final resting place of Civil War general William H. T. Walker, the so-called "Georgia Firebrand."

72

RELIVE THE BOYHOOD
OF A US PRESIDENT

In the years following the Civil War, a new team sport swept the nation, and young boys in Augusta were soon caught up in the fad. Young Woodrow "Tommy" Wilson organized his pals in his downtown neighborhood into the Lightfoot Baseball Club, and the bylaws he established provide perhaps the earliest evidence of the organizational skills of the man who would become our nation's 28th president. One of four house museums dedicated to Wilson's life and career, the three-story red-brick Greek Revival residence celebrates the national leader's first thirteen years. Two floors of this meticulously restored building are open to the public. Many of the furnishings date to the time period when the Wilson family lived in what was then the manse for the Presbyterian church across Telfair Street.

419 Seventh St., 706-722-9828
wilsonboyhoodhome.org

TIP

The offices of Historic Augusta are on the second floor of the adjacent building, the Lamar House, the former home of Wilson's childhood friend and former Lightfoot Baseball Club teammate Joseph Rucker Lamar, who served as a justice of the US Supreme Court from 1910 to 1916. Visit the small gift shop in this building, from which guided tours of the Wilson home generally commence.

GET CLOSE
TO THE TITANIC TRAGEDY

Who can forget the screen romance of Leonardo DiCaprio and Kate Winslet in the 1997 blockbuster movie *Titanic?* DiCaprio plays a fictional hero named Jack Dawson, but Augusta can lay claim to a real-life heroic figure, Archibald Butt, who served as White House military aide during two administrations. Butt was a passenger on the luxury liner during its ill-fated 1912 voyage, and several eyewitness accounts attest to his calm command during the disaster as he supervised some of the evacuation procedures. President William Howard Taft, who regarded Butt as part of his family, was on hand when the city dedicated the Butt Memorial Bridge in 1914. That distinctive hump-backed structure with eagle-topped pillars at each end still spans the canal.

501 15th St.

TIP

See Archibald Butt's portrait in military uniform by friend and similarly doomed passenger Francis Millet. It's part of the permanent collection of the Morris Museum of Art.

COMMUNE
WITH A POPULAR HISTORICAL NOVELIST

The bestseller lists in the middle of the twentieth century often featured books by Frank Yerby, who was born in Augusta in 1911 of African American lineage. His first work to gain critical attention was a short story titled "Health Card," which won the O. Henry Award; it was inspired by an act of racial injustice Yerby himself experienced while a young man in Augusta. His childhood home, which once stood abandoned on Eighth Street, was moved to the campus of Paine College, Yerby's undergraduate alma mater, in 2008. The two-story structure is more of a re-creation than a restoration, but it does boast a fluted staircase and flooring from the original residence. It now serves as the setting for special events, including public programs on Yerby's literary legacy.

Laney Walker Boulevard, Paine College, 706-821-8200
paine.edu

TIP

Yerby published 33 novels. Three of his most popular—*The Foxes of Harrow, The Golden Hawk,* and *The Saracen Blade*—can be enjoyed on both the page and the screen.

75

DISCOVER THE ROOTS
OF A LEGENDARY COMEDY DUO

"Well, here's another fine mess that you've gotten me into" is a catchphrase made popular by the classic comedy duo of Laurel and Hardy. One "mess" or comic predicament after another is at the heart of more than a hundred films, both short and feature-length, that featured both stars. The Laurel and Hardy Museum in Harlem, Georgia, just nineteen miles west of Augusta, commemorates the fact that Oliver Norvell Hardy was born in that small town. Housed in a building that was once a movie theater, the museum contains a host of Laurel and Hardy merchandise and some film props. In the center of one large exhibition space is all the Laurel and Hardy material, and behind that gallery is a thirty-five-seat theater where visitors can view short films by the comedy duo on a continuous loop.

135 Louisville St., Harlem, 706-556-0401
harlemmuseumandwelcomecenter.com

TIP

A great way to be part of the Laurel and Hardy experience is to attend the annual festival in Harlem, now celebrating more than thirty years. Highlights include a parade and a Laurel and Hardy lookalike contest.

FIND ART IN UNEXPECTED PLACES,

SUCH AS THE DENTAL COLLEGE OF GEORGIA

Perhaps the only dental college in the country with a large art gallery, the Dental College of Georgia boasts a 175-piece collection on its five floors. The paintings, sculptures, and fiber art were donated to the institution during the construction of the $112 million facility in 2012. A highlight of any visit is the twenty-eight-foot mosaic chandelier designed by Augusta artist Paul Pearman that hangs suspended from the ceiling of the atrium lobby. Composed of thousands of small tiles of textured and mirrored glass applied to a stainless-steel body, the work titled *The Four Stages of Higher Learning* features four separate tiers, each draped in a seemingly melting surface reminiscent of the liquefied figures in the work of surrealist artist Salvador Dalí.

1430 John Wesley Gilbert Dr., 706-721-2371
augusta.edu/dentalmedicine/about-us/dcgfacility.php

WITNESS HISTORY COME ALIVE IN NORTH AUGUSTA

Commemorating the role of the Augusta area as a trading center during the colonial period, the 7.5-acre Living History Park was established in 1991 on property that once encompassed an abandoned waterworks. In fact, natural springs still run beneath the ground. The site includes a number of replicated eighteenth-century structures, including a grist mill, meeting house, forge, and tavern. The period 1735–85 comes alive during special re-enactment events, including an annual two-day colonial encampment. The site is also ideal for family picnics and recreational walks at any time of year. Be forewarned, however, that the topography is hilly and that to take full advantage of everything the village has to offer, you need to traverse walkways uphill and down.

299 W. Spring Grove Ave., North Augusta, 803-979-9776
colonialtimesus.wordpress.com

TIP

Visit the nearby Sunset Hill Cemetery, which boasts the grave of Berry Greenwood Benson, whose image is featured on top of the Confederate Monument on Broad Street in Augusta. Benson and his brother Blackwood served with bravery in the Confederate army from the firing on Fort Sumter to the end of the war; he escaped twice from Yankee prisons.

VISIT A CHURCH TURNED CULTURAL CENTER:
SACRED HEART

Thanks to the generosity of local philanthropist Peter S. Knox Jr., this former Roman Catholic church opened its doors as a cultural center in 1987. Since that year, Sacred Heart has served as a venue for a variety of public events, most notably the annual Festival of Nine Lessons and Carols and the Garden City Festival. The building itself has long been a city landmark, with its tall twin spires, fifteen kinds of exterior brickwork, and more than ninety stained glass windows. The interior retains its main altar with two kneeling angels, side altars to the Blessed Virgin and St. Joseph, carved Stations of the Cross, a baptistry with display cabinets full of items donated by past congregants, and a choir loft from which visitors can gain a bird's-eye view of the building's impressive proportions.

1301 Greene St., 706-826-4700
sacredheartaugusta.org

TIP

At the center's gift shop, accessible on the 13th Street side, visitors can obtain for a modest fee a thirty-minute, self-guided audio tour of the building, with an emphasis on its history and including the personal stories of those who have played a part in its evolution. Visit on a sunny day when the windows are ablaze with light and color.

79

CELEBRATE
AFRICAN AMERICAN HISTORY

Founded in 1991, the Lucy Craft Laney Museum of Black History celebrates the legacy of its namesake, who established the first school for African American children in Augusta in 1883. In addition to changing exhibitions on a variety of topics and a popular annual craft quilt show, this museum in Laney's former residence showcases several permanent collections, including photographs of notable Black Augustans and artifacts from Augusta-based Pilgrim Health and Insurance Company, which was the first such enterprise established to benefit African Americans in Georgia. Few furnishings from the original house survived a disastrous 1987 fire, but you can still see Laney's beloved piano and other items that were salvaged from the conflagration. The museum often plays host to free public lectures.

1116 Phillips St., 706-724-3576
lucycraftlaneymuseum.com

TIP

After a visit to the Laney Museum, drop by the graves of Augusta's two most notable African American citizens. Graced by a perpetual flame, Laney's burial plot is across the street from the museum on the property of Laney High School. Charles T. Walker's final resting place is just a block away, adjacent to one of the many churches he founded, Tabernacle Baptist Church, which boasts the largest Black congregation in Augusta. The public addresses of this noted late-nineteenth-century orator and evangelist attracted the attention of President William Howard Taft and business magnate John D. Rockefeller.

EXAMINE A PUBLIC SCULPTURE

CREATED IN COLLABORATION WITH LOCAL RESIDENTS

Between Augusta and Summerville once existed the eighteenth-century village of Harrisburg, named after tobacco merchant Ezekiel Harris. The community, which became the locus of cotton manufacturing during the nineteenth century, survived as a distinct entity until the 1870s. To commemorate the past, present, and future of the Harrisburg community, a large public sculpture was erected in A. L. Williams Park on the corner of Broad and Eve streets in 2019. Designed by Larry Millard, the 10.5-foot-tall structure is formed of perforated stainless steel boxes housing objects donated by local residents.

The boxes, twelve on each side with one large box as the crosspiece, form a triumphal arch not unlike those erected by ancient Romans to celebrate military victories. This particular arch, however, serves as a time capsule of sorts, with a host of items contained within. Some have personal significance, such as a skateboard, a tricycle, and a patio chair. Others were salvaged from area businesses and educational institutions, such as textile bobbins from the historic King Mill and bricks and steel from the Martha Lester School.

1850 Broad St., 706-796-5025

81

SURVEY THE HISTORY
OF AUGUSTA'S SISTER CITY ACROSS THE RIVER

Located in the municipal building, the Arts and Heritage Center of North Augusta contains a permanent exhibit on area history and two light-filled galleries for the temporary display of art. The museum, constructed in partnership with the South Carolina National Heritage Corridor, features a well-crafted survey of key developments in the Central Savannah River Area from prehistory to the present. Highlights include a lavish small-scale model crafted by Kelley New and Mike Teffeteller of seventeen notable buildings in North Augusta in 1910. The two-story art gallery is devoted mostly to the work of local artists, including annual competitive exhibitions sponsored by area visual arts organizations. To the left of the entrance is an attractive gift shop. The center is open only on weekdays, the same business hours as the municipal building itself.

100 Georgia Ave., North Augusta, 803-441-4380
artsandheritagecenter.com

TIP

Of particular interest in the permanent history exhibition are informational placards devoted to historic homes in North Augusta, including Elm Grove and Star of Edgefield. Those residences and more can be viewed on a do-it-yourself driving tour of North Augusta, using a printed map sponsored by the local heritage council and available at the municipal building.

STROLL THROUGH THE BYRD GALLERY OF ART

Located on the ground floor of Washington Hall on the Summerville campus of Augusta University, the Mary S. Byrd Gallery of Art has served since 2010 as a great place to sample contemporary art. The gallery, which is essentially one large exhibition space, provides the public with a chance to see recent work by some of the most exciting professional artists active today. It also serves as a laboratory for student learning because the featured artists often provide lectures on their artistic practice, and the works on display add a concrete dimension to the material covered in class. The Byrd Gallery is open only on weekdays except for special events; visitor parking is available between Washington Hall and Reese Library, just off Katherine Street.

2500 Walton Way, 706-667-4888
augusta.edu/byrd

COMMUNE WITH THE SPIRITS
AT MAGNOLIA CEMETERY

Cemeteries are like history books; their many memorials read like pages devoted to memorable figures of the past. No graveyard in Augusta is more resonant than Magnolia Cemetery, which spans sixty acres framed by a brick wall, part of which was fortified for the defense of the city during the Civil War. Highlights include two sections set aside for Civil War combatants. The graves of 337 Confederate soldiers surround a permanent platform erected for memorial events, while nearby rest the remains of 16 Union troops, all prisoners of war who died in the area. Other prominent burials include poets Paul Hamilton Hayne, Richard Henry Wilde, and James Ryder Randall, as well as seven Confederate generals. Especially poignant is the section devoted to the Augusta Orphan Asylum—now the Tuttle-Newton Home. Maps of the full complex are available online.

Main entrance: 702 Third St., 706-821-1746
augustaga.gov/352/magnolia

TIP

Historic Augusta offers an annual tour of the city's oldest cemeteries, in which costumed guides take participants on a "Walk with the Spirits."

84

OGLE THE CITY'S MANY OUTDOOR MURALS

Recently Augusta has enjoyed an explosion of outdoor and indoor wall art. The most notable pieces pay homage to the city's most famous daughters and sons. Opera star Jessye Norman's gift to the world is celebrated by Jay Jacobs's *Girl with Butterflies,* a 30- by 70-foot mural on the exterior wall of the school for the arts that bears Norman's name. The work features a smiling youngster inspired by Norman herself; her red, white, and blue skirt recalls Norman's legendary performance of "La Marseillaise" in Paris as part of the 200th anniversary of the French Revolution in 1989. James Brown's career is celebrated in the monumental, multi-image mural by Cole Phail on the corner of Ninth and Broad.

Jessye Norman School of the Arts: 739 Greene St., 706-828-7768
jessyenormanschool.org

TIP

The greatest assemblage of area murals, all related to the use of water resources, can be found on the walls of the Highland Avenue Water Treatment Plant on Wrightsboro Road.

CHAT WITH A RANGER
AT AN EPICENTER OF KING COTTON

Just across the Savannah River in Beech Island rests the former showcase plantation of one of the South's most iconic antebellum personalities, James Henry Hammond. His ambition did not rest with the accumulation of more and more land and enslaved people; Hammond entered politics, serving South Carolina as both its governor and a US senator. His most famous congressional address included the assertion that "cotton is king." In 1859, Hammond completed the crowning jewel of his cotton empire, Redcliffe Plantation. Now a state historic site, the property includes the Hammond mansion, two slave quarters (one converted into a garage in 1935), a stable, and a new visitor center. Free maps of the park and a free tree guide are available on-site. You can ramble the grounds freely during park hours from 9 a.m. to 6 p.m.

181 Redcliffe Rd., Beech Island, 803-827-1473
southcarolinaparks.com/redcliffe

TIP

Fee-based guided tours can be booked at the visitor center; the public narrative now balances the stories of the Hammond family with those of the generations of enslaved people, sharecroppers, and tenant farmers who worked the land.

SHOPPING AND FASHION

STROLL THROUGH DOWNTOWN ART GALLERIES

Downtown Augusta boasts a number of commercial galleries. The most prestigious is Westobou Gallery, which showcases the work of emerging and mid-career artists, especially those with a focus on experimentation. An offshoot of the annual Westobou festival, the gallery hosts exhibitions not only during that annual fall event but also throughout the year. In direct contrast to Westobou Gallery, which is essentially a stark white box for the display of a few choice pieces, Art on Broad is crammed floor to ceiling with regional arts and crafts. From the reflective glass orbs dangling from the ceiling to the walls covered in paintings and the shelves and cases filled with pottery and jewelry, owner Kristin Varn has created a space that resembles a kaleidoscope of shifting shapes and colors.

Westobou Gallery
1129 Broad St., 706-755-2878
westoboufestival.com

Art on Broad
1028 Broad St., 706-722-1028
facebook.com/artonbroad

TIP

Art on Broad is the best place to find reasonably priced paintings, including small-scale works by local artists such as Jay Jacobs. Inspired by old photographs and images from *National Geographic* magazine, Jacobs generates tiny paintings with alluring appeal, either monochromatic portraits of anonymous personalities or often-whimsical interactions between humans and their animal counterparts.

SATISFY YOUR CRAVING
FOR HAND-BUILT CERAMICS

Located in a former automotive garage, Tire City Potters is one of the city's most welcoming creative spaces, part studio and part gallery. For more than a decade, Tire City Potters has offered the best in thrown ceramic pieces that combine form and function. Owner and lead potter Shishir Chokshi creates his own pieces and also sells the work of other potters and his apprentices. For a unique educational experience, take a pottery class at Tire City. You can build your own mug or master the low-fire process called raku. A graduate of the art program at Augusta University, Chokshi also offers a variety of learning opportunities for children. The most popular is probably the seasonal class on making ceramic pumpkins.

210-B 10th St., 706-294-3871
tcpotters.com

TIP

For an interesting setting for your next party, make a group reservation at Tire City Potters and learn how to throw and fire your own ceramic bowl or mug. The studio is located a stone's throw from a host of fine downtown eateries, so you can combine a class with lunch or dinner.

88

FIND AN OLD FAVORITE
AT THE BOOK TAVERN

Augusta's leading independent bookstore since 2005, the Book Tavern carries new, old, and rare volumes logically organized into various categories. Also on offer is a good selection of signed books and books on local topics. Located across from the New Moon Café in the former JB Whites Building, the single-story space with mezzanine is also fronted by a covered patio where occasional book talks and signings are scheduled. Because everything is so attractively arranged, a visit to the Book Tavern can provide a pleasurable browsing experience. Friendly owner David Hutchison and his staff are happy to special order books. The store has enjoyed various locations in the downtown area since it opened, but each move has been to a larger space. Loyal customers have propelled this positive momentum.

936 Broad St., 706-826-1940
booktavern.com

89

EXPLORE THE FASCINATING HOBBY OF COIN COLLECTING

A life member of the American Numismatic Association, Clein's Rare Coins has been in business since 1941. Founded by Herb Clein, the shop has been run since 2000 by the Damron family. The business specializes in American currency, including Civil War-era currency, but also carries ancient and medieval coins, commemorative medallions, collecting supplies, and reference books. The space is divided into two parts demarcated by a row of display cases: a commercial area in front replete with browsing tables full of often-discounted merchandise and a work area in back. For the coin collector, Clein's is a fun place to drop in for a casual look-see. Because of its constantly rotating inventory, the store always has some new treasure to inspect and some new aspect of numismatic history to explore.

3830 Washington Rd., Martinez, 706-755-2249
cleinsrarecoins.com

90

REVEL IN ALL THINGS OLD
AT THE AREA'S BIGGEST ANTIQUE MARKET

Wear your walking shoes! Boasting 100,000 square feet and more than 175 vendors, the Riverfront Antique Mall offers hours of bargain-hunting pleasure. This converted Kmart is now the biggest such emporium in the Central Savannah River Area. The merchandise is always changing, and you never know what you'll find: everything from vintage glassware to a seven-foot-tall cigar store Indian. Bargaining is acceptable with most of the vendors. There is a café on the premises, serving primarily hamburgers, fries, and baked goods; it is a good place to take a break from what can be a daunting shopping trek.

5979 Jefferson Davis Hwy., North Augusta, 803-279-0900
riverfrontantiquemallsc.com

91

SELECT NON-TRADITIONAL FASHION

FOR WEDDINGS AND OTHER FORMAL EVENTS

Some occasions call for dressing up. Sho Ane's Design Studio has long been a ladies' fashion fixture in downtown Augusta. For thirty years, Sho Ane Seaton has been crafting one-of-a-kind bridal and formal wear. Her talented staff, rated highly for their customer service skills, can also size and alter pieces by other designers carried by the studio, such as Jovani and Mori Lee. Formal wear for men and children can also be found on-site, and loyal customers happily anticipate the regularly scheduled sales.

314 E Martintown Rd., North Augusta, 706-724-7220

TIP

Sho Ane and her husband, John Seaton, have also opened a new café in downtown Augusta, just around the corner from her design studio. The Cyber Bistro on Reynolds Street is open for breakfast, lunch, and dinner. Try the turkey avocado melt or the roasted red pepper and avocado spread on toast.

92

LUXURIATE

IN THE FINEST MEN'S CLOTHING

At the top of most local surveys regarding classic men's clothing and sportswear are two special retailers, known not only for their fine merchandise but also for their attentive customer service. A classic men's clothier since 1963 is Gentry Men's Shop in Surrey Center. From top to toe, this haberdashery offers the finest in men's clothing and accessories. Equally popular is Boardroom Clothing Company, which opened its doors in 1988; this emporium carries a wide assortment of attire for formal, corporate, and casual occasions. The staffs at both stores pride themselves on developing cordial relationships with their customers.

Gentry Men's Shop
451 Highland Ave., Surrey Center
706-733-2256, gentrymensshop.com

Boardroom Clothing Company
3604 Verandah Dr., 706-733-6203
boardroomaugusta.com

EXPLORE
THE CITY'S LARGEST JEWELRY RETAILER

One of the biggest independent jewelry enterprises in the country, Windsor Fine Jewelers has long been a staple for those who crave the largest selection of rings and watches in the Central Savannah River Area. Since 1975, three generations of the Thompson family have managed this two-story emporium, which is known especially for its fine collections in the following designer lines: distinctive diamond-encrusted gold and silver pieces by Roberto Coin; Balinese-inspired, eco-friendly gold and silver pieces by John Hardy, and earrings and necklaces featuring Mikimoto cultured pearls. The staff are skilled at repairing and restoring jewelry items that patrons hold dear.

2635 Washington Rd., 706-738-7777
windsorfinejewelers.com

PICK THE PERFECT POSEY
AT MARTINA'S FLOWERS AND GIFTS

Some people are proficient in the language of flowers. Since 1975, Martina's has been serving the floral needs of the Augusta community. Specialties include wedding flowers, sympathy arrangements, bouquets for corporate events, and wholesale/bulk orders. Its large commercial space boasts not only cut flowers and potted plants but also an assortment of stuffed toys and even a candy counter. It's a fun place to browse for that perfect gift for a special occasion. Rated highly for their friendly customer service and reliable delivery, Martina's has long been the leading florist shop in Augusta.

3925 Washington Rd., 706-863-7172
martinas.com

TIP

If you waited until the last minute to pick a present or you are panicking over the right hostess gift for that imminent dinner party, relax! Martina's has weekly grab-and-go specials.

95

COMPARE YOUR TASTE
WITH GRANNIE'S

Some may call it a junk shop; others rate it near the top of their list for finding just the right vintage item to complete their personal collection. Located in a former residential building, Mema Had One has a warren of small rooms crammed with some antiques and even more collectibles. The store is named after the grandmother of co-owner Pam Hayes, who along with her two partners began the business by decorating restaurants with old-time items. Not only is the interior crammed with quaint and curious items, the backyard is generally full of architectural salvage. Many area residents regularly drop by to see what's new.

2328 Washington Rd., 706-421-0626
memahadone.net

96

SEARCH FOR BARGAINS
AT CONSIGNMENT SHOPS

Sometimes a "gently owned" secondhand item is the best, most cost-effective option. Especially in the case of designer clothing, savvy shoppers have learned to browse at consignment shops, where prices are often a third of what they might be at a traditional retail shop. Like any other municipality of a certain size, Augusta has its fair share of consignment shops. Among the best are Second Time Around, which offers a fine range of clothing, furniture, and home decor, and Consign Design, which specializes in fine furniture.

Second Time Around
3690 Washington Rd., 706-863-1094
staconsignments.com

Consign Design
318 Baston Rd., 706-945-0176

TIP

Take advantage of the popular $1 sale the first Tuesday of every month at Second Time Around.

97

LEARN MORE ABOUT VINTAGE CLOTHING

AT VINTAGE OOOLLEE

Since 2008, discriminating buyers in search of vintage clothing have turned to local expert Caren Dorn Bricker. Her shop, Vintage Ooollee, carries a good selection of clothes and accessories for men, women, and children. Also on offer are costumes for a variety of occasions and new wardrobe items with a retro vibe. Located on upper Broad Street in the heart of downtown Augusta, Vintage Ooollee is a good bet for one-of-a-kind outfits, especially for theme parties and events. The store also sponsors makeup tutorials. The retail space is deceptively large, divided into two parts. Vintage clothing and accessories can be found in the large room just inside the main entrance; to the left is another sizable chamber with a host of costume racks, a wall of wigs, and a makeup counter.

1121 Broad St., 706-724-2591

98

EMBRACE THE MALL EXPERIENCE
AT AUGUSTA MALL

Although the golden age of the shopping mall is long gone, the brick-and-mortar retail experience that is Augusta Mall is still going strong. With nearly 150 stores, Augusta Mall remains a top-flight shopping destination. Spread out over two floors in the main building, with additional commercial establishments in an adjoining pedestrian shopping area, Augusta Mall includes some of the nation's biggest chains as well as smaller retailers. Visitors can ramble through major department stores such as Macy's and Dillard's and also browse specialty shops selling everything from Apple phones to Italian Capodimonte porcelain. If you are in the mood to spend the day at the mall, there is a food court as well as sit-down restaurants such as P.F. Chang's, The Chop House, and Crab Du Jour.

3450 Wrightsboro Rd., 706-550-6657
augustamall.com

TIP

If time is of the essence,
many of the mall stores provide curbside service.

FIND YOUR NEXT UNEXPECTED TREASURE AT AREA FLEA MARKETS

The French are credited with having coined the term *flea market* because the secondhand articles once sold at such mercantile establishments were often infested with the parasites. Visitors to the two major flea markets in South Augusta need have no fear that the goods they purchase will come with unwelcome guests. Augusta is one of five cities to host a Barnyard Flea Market; the local franchise has six-hundred retail spots organized around a central hallway, with six perpendicular causeways on each side. For more than forty years, the Rhodes family has operated the South Augusta Flea Market, largely rebuilt after a disastrous fire about ten years ago. This smaller market houses about two hundred vendors, with used furniture as the principal offering. For children and teens, the family operates a Sunday school in a miniature schoolhouse.

Barnyard Flea Market
1625 Doug Barnard Pkwy.
706-793-8800
barnyardfleamarkets.com

South Augusta Flea Market
1562 Doug Barnard Pkwy.
706-798-5500
southaugustafleamarketinc.com

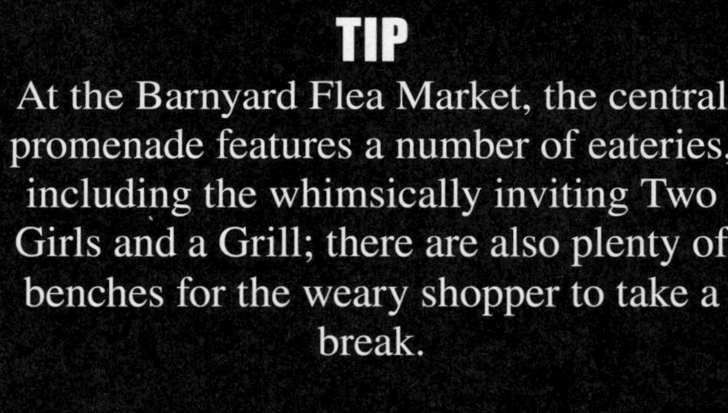

TIP

At the Barnyard Flea Market, the central promenade features a number of eateries, including the whimsically inviting Two Girls and a Grill; there are also plenty of benches for the weary shopper to take a break.

100

GO FRESH
AT THE AUGUSTA MARKET

Satirist P. J. O'Rourke once wrote that "vegetables are something God invented to let women get even with their children." If you were not scared off by greens in your childhood, the Central Savannah River Area has a number of options for finding fresh local produce. One of the most popular is the Saturday market near the Riverwalk, held every weekend from March to November. Vendors sell fruits, vegetables, and baked goods as well as art and jewelry; the number of stalls can vary considerably from week to week and depending on the weather. Exploring the market can offer a pleasant outdoor experience for the whole family; pets are welcome too.

15 Eighth St., 706-627-0128
theaugustamarket.com

For the exercise-minded, the market is the Saturday morning meeting place for group jogs. Under the label of the Triple 8 Run, participants can choose one-, two-, or three-mile options during market season.

ACTIVITIES BY SEASON

SPRING

SUMMER

FALL

WINTER

SUGGESTED ITINERARIES

DOWNTOWN ARTS SCENE

RAMBLES AND RIDES

DOWNTOWN HISTORY WALKS

FUN FOR CHILDREN

CROSSING THE RIVER

ADVENTURES ON WATER

SPECTATOR THRILLS

RANGING OVER THE HILL

INDEX

1794
EMILY TUBMAN
1885